MASTERING YOUR MONEY

Table of Contents

MASTERING YOUR MONEY

Chapter 1

Jesus Christ gave us thirty-eight parables. Sixteen of those thirty-eight parables deal with money management. Do you realize that more is said in the New Testament about money than heaven and hell combined?

Five times more is said about money than prayer. There are five hundred verses on both prayer and faith, yet there are over two thousand verses dealing with money and possessions.

The fact is that you will either master your money, or your money will master you. Who wouldn't want God to explode their prosperity? Who wouldn't like the windows of heaven to open and for God to bless them with blessings they could not contain?

Deuteronomy 8:18, "But remember the Lord your God, for it is He who gives you the ability to produce wealth."

Principle #1

You will never prosper until you believe and confess that it is God's will for you to prosper!

It is God's will for you to prosper. If God blessed Abraham with lavish prosperity, He can pour blessings of prosperity upon you that you will be unable to contain. You must confess His Word for your prosperity!

3 John 1:2, "Beloved I wish above all else that you prosper and be in good health, even as your soul prospers."

1 Chronicles 29:12, "Both riches and honor come of Thee O God for You reign over all the earth..."

Psalm 1:1-3, "Blessed is the man that walketh not in the counsel of the ungodly, nor standeth in the way of sinners, nor sitteth in the seat of the scornful... And he shall be like a tree planted by the rivers of water, that bringeth forth his fruit in his season; his leaf also shall not wither; and whatsoever he doeth shall prosper."

Principle #2

God owns all the wealth in the world!

Matthew 25:14, "For the kingdom of heaven is as a man traveling to a far country, who called his own servants and delivered unto them his goods."

There are two revolutionary implications in this verse: First, it is God's money and He has the right to whatever He wants. As the owner he has rights; as the steward I have responsibilities. Second, since all my money is God's money, every spending decision I make is a spiritual decision. Your checkbook is a spiritual reflection of your love for Christ.

You are a steward, while God is the owner. You will give an account to God for how you managed His resources.

Principle #3

All of God's wealth belongs to His children!

You do not qualify for God's abundance until you become God's child. You cannot pray "Our Father which art in heaven" until you receive Jesus.

The Bible says, "No man cometh unto the Father but by Me."

There are two families in the Bible: The family of God ("Our Father which art in heaven") and the family of Satan (Jesus said, "Ye are of your father the devil"). When God is your father, all His wealth belongs to you. He has promised to take care of His children. So with the question: Why are people in India starving? The answer is: God is not their father. Their God is a cow or rat.

1 Corinthians 3:21-23, "Therefore let no man glory in men. For all things are yours… and ye are Christ's and Christ is God's."

Romans 8:17 declares, "And if children, then heirs; heirs of God and joint-heirs with Christ". Not equal heirs (half and half), but joint-heirs. All that He has is yours, and all that you have is His.

At Calvary, I brought to Him my poverty, and He brought the riches of Abraham. When Jesus was on the cross, He was hungry, thirsty, and naked. When He died, He was buried in a borrowed tomb, but when He cried, "It is finished!" poverty died. I was a Gentile, and he adopted me and made me a child of the King. I now have the royal blood of heaven flowing in my veins. I am saved, sealed, and sanctified.

Principle #4

The difference between living a life of prosperity and a life of poverty is a matter of choice!

Deuteronomy 30:19, "...I have set before you life and death, blessing and cursing; therefore, choose life." Blessing is a result of choice.

Luke 6:38, "Give, and it shall be given unto you; good measure, pressed down, and shaken together, and running over." The fact is that givers gain, but you have to make the choice to be a giver. If you are not receiving it, it's because you are not giving it. The Word says to "give, and it shall be given unto you". Should you expect to gain when you give? Yes!

Tithing is a choice. If you choose to not tithe, you will be living under a financial curse. What is your choice? Would you rather be blessed by Almighty God or live under a curse?

Diligence is also a choice. Proverbs 13:4 says, "The soul of the sluggard desireth and hath nothing; but the soul of the diligent shall be made fat." What does this mean? Go to work! The only place you find success before work is in the dictionary. God provides worms for birds, but He doesn't shove them down their throats. Fight poverty the American way... get a job! Your financial prosperity tomorrow will be determined by your obedience today. It is your choice!

God's children have historically been prosperous. In Genesis 13, Abraham is described as having many cattle along with silver and gold. This description is not of being spiritually rich, but of being "literally" rich. Solomon was wealthy.

Archaeologists have discovered that Solomon had hinges on his horse stables that were gold plated. King David said, "The Lord is my shepherd, I shall not want." That was a confession of prosperity. David gave one hundred million for the building of the temple. That is not too bad for someone who started out with five rocks and a slingshot.

The doctrine of Popini in the Middle Ages stated, "Poverty is spiritual". That is not so! Poverty is a curse that is a result of sin. Sin produces poverty. One drunk driver can instantly change the lives of a carload of healthy, happy people. AIDS brings poverty, drug addiction brings poverty, alcoholism brings poverty, and crime brings poverty. There is a high price for low living... the wages of sin is death.

Principle #5

Jesus proclaimed His personal wealth!

If wealth were a negative thing, why would God the Father give it to His Son, Jesus Christ? Revelation 5:12, "Worthy is the Lamb that was slain to receive power, and riches, and wisdom, and strength, and honor, and glory and blessing!" These seven blessings are given to the Son and to the Church.

Matthew 13:44 says, "The kingdom of heaven is like a treasure hidden in a field..." Treasure excites people. John the Revelator described his eternal home as having foundations of twelve kinds of precious stones, twelve gates of solid pearl, and streets made of gold.

Mansions have been designed by the Architect of the Ages for God's children.

People like to say that Jesus was poor. When was He poor? Jesus was poor while He was on the cross. Why was He poor on the cross? He was poor, because He took the poverty of those who accepted Him and replaced it with the wealth of Abraham.

Principle #6

God wants you to invest in yourself!

"Lay up for yourself treasures in heaven." The day is going to come when all you will have is what you have given to God. There are two words that Christians tend to confuse: self-interest (which is good) and selfishness (which is a spiritual cancer).

It is in my self-interest to be saved. The options are heaven and hell. It is in my self-interest to be happy. The Bible says, "A merry heart doeth good like a medicine" and "The joy of the Lord is my strength." It is in your self-interest to invest in the Kingdom of God, because God controls the economy on both sides of the Jordan River.

Matthew 19:29, "And everyone that hath forsaken houses, or brethren, or sisters or father or mother or wife or children or lands for my sake shall receive one hundred fold in this life and shall inherit everlasting life." What is the rate of return on one hundred fold? One hundred fold has a return of ten thousand percent. The Kingdom of God pays ten thousand percent, so it is in your self-interest to invest all you can get your hands on.

Principle #7

Jesus taught us to invest wisely by investing in things that are permanent!

Jesus taught us that it is not in our self-interests to invest in something that moths can eat, rust can decay, or that thieves can carry off. Dewdrops are as pretty as diamonds until the sun comes out, because they are not permanent. The Bible teaches us that the world shall pass away. Simply said, the earth is not permanent.

2 Peter 3:10, "But the day of the Lord will come as a thief in the night in which the heavens shall pass away with a great noise and the elements shall melt with a fervent heat and the earth also and the works that are therein shall be burned up."

You need to invest wisely in the Kingdom of God. Lay up treasures for yourselves and invest in the Gospel!

Principle #8

Why give? God has created a universe where it is impossible to receive without giving!

The fact is that everything that God controls gives. If something within you resents giving, that something is not of God. Giving is the only proof you have that greed has not become a cancer on your soul.

The sun gives light without which the world would cease. The plants give food, and the clouds give rain. God the Father so loved the world that He gave His only begotten Son. Givers gain. You do not qualify to receive from God or anyone else until you give.

The Bible commands, "Give and it shall be given unto you." Until you give you will not qualify to receive the power to get wealth.

Principle #9

God Almighty controls the economy of America... and God controls your income!

Your source is God, not the United States' government. The Bible says, "It is the Lord that giveth the power to get wealth." When you give to God, He controls your income. There is no such thing as fixed income in the Kingdom of God. Your income is controlled by your giving.

A widow in the Old Testament gave her last piece of bread to Elijah. After that she and her son prepared to die of starvation. This was a time of great depression. She was a single parent, and Elijah had asked for her last slice of bread. She gave it to him. As soon as she gave what was in her hand, God supernaturally caused the cruse of oil to fill and the barrel to fill that were in her home. At that point she had more than she could use. She had supernatural abundance, and that is what God wants for you.

How do you get it? When you let go of what is in your hands towards God, then God will let go of what is in His hands towards you. The decision to live in poverty or prosperity is yours. Your future financial condition will be determined by your obedience. God is not limited to what you have. He is limited by what you give.

Principle #10

Two kinds of givers: reason givers and revelation givers!

Reason givers are controlled by their minds. They do not ask God how much they should give; they ask their CPA.

Revelation givers are controlled by the Holy Spirit. They see God as their supplier. Revelation givers do not give according to what they have, but according to what God can supply. Revelation givers know that the earth is going to pass away and know the true value of a soul.

It is important to remember that as soon as you do something special for God, there is always someone saying that you did wrong. Matthew 26 tells the story of Mary. She broke an alabaster box with twelve ounces of precious ointment over the head and body of Jesus as a memorial of her love. Judas yelled out that she had wasted a year's wages on it and that the money could have been used to feed and clothe the poor. Jesus said that wherever the Gospel was preached in the whole world "what this woman has done will be a memorial for her."

Remember it is the Lord who gives you the power to get wealth. Give and it shall be given unto you. God has given you His very best, will you give Him yours?

MASTERING YOUR MONEY

Chapter 2

Everything God does on earth comes from the principle of seedtime and harvest. Genesis 8:22, "While the earth remains, seedtime and harvest, and cold and heat, and summer and winter, and day and night shall not cease."

Consider the spiritual realm. How did Jesus Christ come to earth? The answer: seedtime and harvest. Genesis 3:15, "The seed of a woman shall crush the head of the serpent." The Holy Ghost planted seed into Mary's womb, and the kingdom of Satan was defeated.

Consider the physical realm. How did you get here? The answer: seedtime and harvest. These two events were separated by nine months.

Consider the financial realm. Luke 6:38 states, "Give and it shall be given unto you." What is the "it" that you have planted? If you plant an apple seed, you will get apples. If you plant a peach seed, you will get peaches. If you plant finances, you will get finances. The Bible says that whatsoever a man soweth that shall he also reap.

You must be careful of what you

plant. You will reap what you sow. If you sow wild oats, you will reap them. If you take action, you will reap what you sow.

Principle #1

Giver's Gain!

If you give to the Lord, you should be expecting a gain! "Give and it shall be given unto you, good measure, pressed down, shaken together and running over." (Luke 6:38) Every time God gives you an opportunity to give, He is also giving you an opportunity to increase your income.

Some of you think that because you are so far behind financially, that you will never catch up. That is wrong. God is able to make it up to you by giving you everything you need and more so that there will not only be enough for your needs but plenty left over to give joyfully to others. Your only hope of catching up is planting seed in the Kingdom of God. The Kingdom of God is the only surefire investment you will ever have.

Principle #2

You must plant your seed before you can expect an increase!

The Bible says, "There is a time to plant and a time to pluck up that which is planted." (Eccl. 3:2) Without seedtime it is impossible to have a harvest. If you give nothing, you get nothing. God can increase what you give one hundred fold, but nothing times nothing equals nothing.

Jesus said (John 12:24), "Verily I say unto you, except a corn of wheat fall into the ground…it abideth alone, it does no good." When what you have in your hand is not enough to meet your need it becomes your seed. You can do three things with seed: eat it, feed it to your cows, or plant it. The fact is that there is no chance of increase until you plant it. You cannot have financial freedom without increase, and you cannot have increase without first planting your seed.

Many people say, "I have nothing to give." That is wrong. 2 Corinthians 9:10-11, "God who gives seed to farmers to plant will give you more and more seed to plant and will make it grow so you can give away more and more fruit from your harvest." You do not have to understand God's economic system for it to work. Isaiah 55:8-9, "My thoughts are not your thoughts, neither are your ways My ways saith the Lord. For as the heavens are higher than the earth so are My ways higher than your ways and My thoughts higher than your thoughts." When you plant your seed in the Kingdom of God, the Lord will multiply it far better than Wall Street.

What causes an economic crash? Hoarding. People stop investing their money because they develop a lack of confidence. The economy then freezes up and that is followed by a recession and crash.

In God's economic system, He gives to you so you can give to others. The money in God's system is constantly in circulation. His economy can never crash. Plant your money into the Kingdom of God. That is when you become wealthy enough to have financial freedom.

Principle #3

Tithe is not a debt we owe; it is a seed we sow!

Tithe is ten percent of your income. Do I expect you to give ten percent of your income to God? No I don't, but He does. He controls your income.

Leviticus 27:30, "All the tithe of the land, whether of the seed of the land or of the fruit of the tree, is the Lord's." Are you giving what is right, or what is left? Malachi 3:10, "Bring ye all the tithes into the storehouse." Not some, ALL!

The fact is that you do not use your electricity and pay the water company. You pay your tithes where you are spiritually fed. Why tithe? The Lord commands it. Refusal to tithe is rebellion against God. If you do not tithe, you live under a financial curse. Malachi 3:9 states, "You are cursed with a curse for you have robbed Me."

Prosperity is a decision. You tithe because God will give to you an increase of income when you do. Malachi 3:10, "Prove Me now says the Lord of Hosts. If I will not open the windows of heaven and pour out on you blessings that there will not be room enough to receive."

Principle #4

You determine the size of your harvest when you sow your seed!

Do you need a big harvest? Sow a lot of seed. 2 Corinthians 9:6, "He which soweth sparingly shall reap also sparingly, and he which soweth bountifully shall reap also bountifully."

"For with the same measure that you use in giving it will be measured back to you." (Luke 6:38) Everyone agrees that prosperity is better than poverty. What most people don't realize is that it is your choice. You determine the size of your harvest when the offering pan comes by. Plant your seed according to your need. Attack your lack with seedtime and harvest.

Your prosperity gives God pleasure. "Let the Lord be magnified which has pleasure in the prosperity of His servant." (Psalm 35:7) The Bible also says that God wishes above all things that you prosper and be in good health. God rejoices when His children receive wealth. If you are not prospering, it is not God's fault. If you are not receiving, then you are not giving.

Principle #5

Plant your seed in good ground!

What is good ground? Good ground is the Kingdom of God. Jesus said, "Seek ye first the Kingdom of God and all these things shall be added unto you."

The fact is that not every church is good ground. Not every television ministry is good ground. Why? Many churches and ministries do not represent the true Kingdom of God.

A church that ordains homosexuals into the ministry, denies the virgin birth or denies the inspired Word of God does not represent the true Kingdom of God. Any church or ministry that supports abortion does not represent the true Kingdom of God. The Bible says that abortion is death. Any television ministry that promotes positive thinking over repentance and confession to Jesus Christ our Lord and Savior is preaching a false doctrine and therefore does not represent the true Kingdom of God.

Principle #6

Be patient! You must wait for the harvest!

"Be not slothful but a follower of them who through faith and patience inherit the promises." (Hebrews 6:12) "The good ground are they, which in an honest and good heart bring forth fruit with patience." (Luke 8:15)

Many of you plant your seed abundantly in good ground but kill your harvest, because you are impatient.

"If we hope for that which we see not, then do we with patience wait for it." (Romans 8:25) "For ye have need of patience, that after you have done the will of God, you might receive the promise." (Hebrews 10:36) "Let us not be weary in well doing, for in due season we shall reap if we faint not." (Galatians 6:9)

Esau sold his birthright for a bowl of potage because of impatience. His impatience killed his harvest. If you invest one thousand dollars in the Kingdom of God through your church offering, do not look for the one hundred-fold return before you leave that morning. Impatience will kill your harvest.

You can also kill your harvest by murmuring. Mark 11:23, "For verily I say unto you, that whosoever shall say unto this mountain, 'Be thou removed and cast into the sea' he shall have whatsoever he saith."

Murmuring sounds like this: "God's not going to come through this time; I've waited long enough; Where is God when you really need Him." Murmuring will cause God to cancel your harvest. When

Israel murmured against God, He sent snakes to bite them. The snake is the symbol of Satan. When you murmur, you are inviting snakes to enter your life. You are inviting Satan and his demon power to destroy your harvest.

Principle #7

The decision to live in poverty or prosperity is yours!

Deuteronomy 30:19, "I call heaven and earth to record this day against you, that I have set before you life and death, blessings and cursing, therefore choose life that both thou and thy seed may live."

Obedience is the equal of prosperity, while disobedience results in a curse. Which do you choose?

Principle #8

God is trying to establish His kingdom on earth!

We talk mostly about God getting us into heaven, but the Bible teaches us that God is trying to establish His kingdom on earth. The Lord's Prayer states, "Thy kingdom come, Thy will be done on earth as it is in heaven." God sought to establish His kingdom in the Garden of Eden, but Adam and Eve disobeyed. They went from abundance to lack. God then sought to dwell with man in the Tabernacle in the wilderness. God lived in the Holy of Holies, and there was not one sick or feeble among them. God's presence filled Solomon's temple until men could not stand in the presence of God.

"I, John, saw the Holy City coming

down out of heaven from God and I heard a loud voice from heaven saying, 'Behold, the Tabernacle of God is with men and He will dwell with them'..."

From Genesis to Revelation, God has been trying to get heaven into earth. Heaven has nothing but staggering abundance, and God wants His kingdom principles to rule the earth. Why hasn't it? We have rejected His principle of seedtime and harvest.

Principle #9

Hard times are wrong times to stop giving to God!

You give your way out of financial lack. In Psalm 37:25 David said, "I have been young and now I am old, yet I have never seen the righteous forsaken nor His seed begging for bread."

Dr. Cho's church in Korea has five hundred thousand members. How did they finance their building program? It started with one woman bringing her rice bowl and laying it at the altar of the church. The congregation then followed. The congregation's seed allowed such a large harvest that they built the church with cash.

Principle #10

If it were sinful for you to enjoy material blessings then God would not have given them to Abraham, Isaac, Jacob, David, Solomon or His Son Jesus Christ!

Revelation 5:12, "Worthy is the Lamb who was slain to receive power, and riches, and wisdom, and strength, and honor and glory and blessing."

The prayer of Jabez (1 Chronicles 4:10) says, "And Jabez called upon the God of Israel saying: 'O that You would bless me, and enlarge my territory that Your hand would be with me, that You would keep me from evil that I might be free from pain'." What was God's response? God granted Jabez his request.

When you turn loose of what is in your hand to God, God will turn loose of what is in His hand to you.

MASTERING YOUR MONEY

Chapter 3

Money is an exciting topic. If you mention the word it will cause people's blood pressure to raise, nostrils to flare, and perspiration will roll down their foreheads.

You have been reading about Bible principles in mastering your money. Before I introduce new principles, I want to review a few.

Giver's gain

You must understand the principles of farming to understand God's principle of seedtime and harvest. Jesus said, "Behold a sower went out to sow… the seed fell on good ground and brought forth fruit." (Matthew 13:3-8)

You must plant your seed

If there is no seedtime, there can be no harvest time. If you did not send your ship out, don't look for your ship to come in.

Tithe

You must tithe because God commands it. If you do not tithe you will live under God's economic curse. Malachi 3:9, "You are cursed with a curse."

You determine the size of your harvest

You determine the size of your harvest when you sow your seed. Do you need a big harvest? Sow lots of seed.

Plant your seed in good ground

Not every ministry is good ground. Not every church represents the Kingdom of God. Investing in ministries whose ground is not good is like throwing seed on an asphalt parking lot.

You must be patient

You must wait for the harvest. Two things can kill your harvest: impatience and murmuring.

Principle #1

God gives you wealth not to hoard it, but to be a blessing to other people!

We plant by reaching out to others and then reap as God reaches out to us. God said to Abraham, "I will bless you and you shall be a blessing."

Abraham is our spiritual father. Galatians 3:29 states, "If ye be in Christ, then are ye Abraham's seed and his heir according to the promise."

If your spiritual father is wealthy, if it is your divine assignment to be a blessing- then how can you fulfill God's commission to be a blessing without abundance? How can you feed the poor, clothe the naked, build churches or a television ministry if you cannot clothe and feed yourself?

The fact is if you are serving a God limited in finances then you are not serving the God of Abraham, Isaac, and Jacob. Haggai 2:8, "The silver is mine and the gold is mine, saith the Lord of Hosts."

It is a blessing to walk up to a home where a family is carrying out their possessions, who cannot pay their rent, and pay their rent for them. How can you do that without abundance? God gives you wealth to bless other people, not so you can live like King Tut, but so you can bless others. "You ask and do not receive because you ask with wrong motives, so that you may spend it on your pleasures." (James 4:3)

Wealth is given to those who make evangelism a top priority. Deuteronomy 8:18 declares, "Remember the Lord thy

God, for it is He that gives power to get wealth, that He may confirm His covenant which He swore to your fathers as it is this day."

Principle #2

Change your attitude about abundance to receive abundance!

Your thoughts determine your destiny. You can live life without limit or live life on your pity pot. It is your choice.

Some people have a poverty complex. It goes like this: Jesus was poor. I am poor. I am like Jesus. That is wrong; Jesus wasn't poor.

Jesus had a nice house. John 1:38-39 states, "Jesus turned and saw them following Him and said unto them, 'What seek ye?' They said, 'Rabbi, where dwellest thou?' Jesus said, 'Come and see'; they came and saw where He dwelt and abode with Him that day." The fact is that the house was big enough to hold that crowd.

Jesus wore the finest clothes. John 19:23 states that Jesus had a seamless robe. It was so valuable that the Roman soldiers gambled it at Calvary. Jesus had enough money that He assigned one of His disciples to carry the bag. That is not poor!

If you are walking around with your lower lip trembling saying Jesus was poor; I am poor, and that makes me spiritual because I am like Jesus, you are wrong and in deception.

Wake up and smell the coffee. You don't understand the principles of seedtime and harvest. God wants to give you wells you did not dig, vineyards you didn't plant, and open the windows of heaven and pour out a blessing you cannot contain.

Some people feel guilty about having nice things. Jesus didn't; he enjoyed nice things. He does not care how many things you own as long as the things do not own you. It is not about possessions; it is about priorities. God demands to be first.

Principle #3

God's purpose produces God's power for financial freedom!

You will not have God's power or His prosperity until you find God's purpose for your life. God has a purpose for your life. You need to find it.

"And we know that all things work together for good to those who love God, to them who are called according to His purpose." (Romans 8:28)

God said to Elijah, "Go to the house of the widow woman; I will feed you there." God had an exact place for Elijah to serve. He also has an exact place for you to serve. If you find that place for you to serve, you will find His power, His provision, and a supernatural abundance.

How many of you have lived in a land of not enough or just enough? How many of you would prefer to live in the promised land of more than enough? The fact is you cannot get to the Promised Land without first leaving Egypt. You have to give up what you have to get what God wants to give you. Good is the enemy of better, and better is the enemy of best.

If you are in Egypt or the wilderness, start marching toward the Promised Land. You are Abraham's seed, and he didn't live on just enough. Break out of your wilderness complex – out of mediocrity and into magnificence. Attack your lack with seedtime and harvest. Reach for life without limit in the Promised Land.

Get a new attitude, believe for a financial breakthrough, and press toward the Land flowing with milk and honey. God wants to shower you with abundance, but He can't as long as you stay in Egypt.

Principle #4

Release the anointing on your finances!

"And it shall come to pass in that day

that his burden shall be taken away from thy shoulder, and his yoke from thy neck, and the yoke will be destroyed because of the anointing oil." (Isaiah 10:27)

What is the anointing? The anointing removes burdens and destroys yokes (Isaiah 10:27). If burdens are not removed and yokes not destroyed, they were not anointed.

Principle #5

Release God's anointing to get out of debt!

God can supernaturally bless your finances to help you get out of debt. You will never have financial freedom if you allow yourself to be trapped in the quick-sand of debt.

Debt is not a sin, but it is dangerous.

Proverbs 22:7, "The borrower is servant (slave) to the lender." Many of you are slaves to banks. You must learn the most important sentence in human speech: I cannot afford it.

There are three questions you need to ask yourself before buying anything: Do I need this; Does my spouse agree with me about making this debt; and How am I going to pay this back?

Debt destroys your relationship to God. You sink yourself into debt, lose your job, and get bitter at God because your home gets repossessed. The fact is that debt creates another god, the banker. If we came before God with the same humility with which we go see the banker, revival would explode in America.

Plant your seed according to your need. Break the debt bondage. You will not get out of debt overnight, but you will little by little.

Principle #6

The final step to financial freedom is to place your seed in anointed hands!

How do you get your not enough turned into more than enough? John 6:9-14 tells the story of a little boy who has five barley loaves and two small fish. Jesus needed to feed 5000 people, and He turned to this young boy who gladly gave his lunch (seed). The young boy placed it in the hands of anointed hands (Jesus), and those hands multiplied it at least fifteen thousand times. The boy then went home with twelve baskets full of leftovers.

They started with not enough and they ended with more than enough.

When you put your seed in anointed hands, God will multiply it supernaturally beyond your wildest dreams.

MASTERING YOUR MONEY

Chapter 4

The name "Jabez" is a synonym for pain.

His own mother said, "Because I bore him in pain." This is not the pain of childbirth, it is a greater pain not mentioned in the text.

Pain drove Jabez to seek a better life. Many of you suffer from inner pain: The pain of a bitter divorce, bankruptcy, betrayal, rejection, unexpected tragedy, or a health crisis.

Jesus Christ is a portrait of pain. Isaiah said, "He is a man of sorrows and acquainted with grief." Jesus had the pain of being illegitimate, a homeless refugee, a hated minority, being oppressed by the government, slandered by the religious leaders, betrayed by His friends, and ultimately by death on the cross.

The secret of living a great life is transforming tragedy into triumph. Forget what is behind you. St. Paul said (Phil. 3:13-14), "Forgetting those things which are behind and reaching forth unto those things which are before, I press toward the mark for the prize of the high calling of God in Christ Jesus."

You must remember that life is a road-not a parking lot. Life is a battle-not a rest home. Life is a school-not a cemetery. Move on beyond your adversities and acrimony. Move forward beyond your tragedies and tears. Move past your setbacks and suffering.

Helen Keller moved beyond the pain of blindness to inspire the world with academic genius. Beethoven moved beyond the pain of deafness and wrote masterful music the world still loves to hear. Abraham Lincoln moved beyond the pain of a nervous breakdown and eleven political defeats to become the greatest President of the United States of America.

St. Paul wrote (2 Corinthians 4:8),

"We are hard pressed on every side, yet not crushed; we are perplexed, but not in despair, persecuted, but not abandoned, struck down, but not destroyed..." ,we are more than conquerors through Christ our Lord.

Jesus Christ moved beyond the pain of Calvary to the joyous shout of the Resurrection morning. Jesus said, "Be of good cheer, I have overcome the world."

Jabez moved beyond the unspoken pain of his youth to reach for a life without limit. He wanted a life more abundant, that was super-charged with miracle power. Jabez wanted a life by faith, not by sight. He got that life.

Whatever the pain of your past or present, it is not nearly as great as your future. What you have been through is not as important as what you are going to do. Your past is over. Today is the best day of the rest of your life. The Bible declares, "Weeping may endure for the night, but joy cometh in the morning."

Job 8:7, "Your beginnings will seem humble so prosperous will your future be." Jeremiah 29:11, "For I know the plans I have for you, declares the Lord, plans to prosper you and not to harm you, plans to give you hope and a future." Isaiah 45:2-3, "I will go before you and make the crooked places straight; I will break in pieces the gates of brass and cut in sunder the bars of iron... I will give you treasure and hidden riches that you may know that I am the Lord."

Jabez asked God to help him live life without limit! "Oh that you would enlarge my territory"

The resurrection story is a story of

life without limit. From the Genesis of time man looked at death as the ultimate end, the limit-but when Jesus died-He rose from the grave and defeated death, hell, and the grave.

Because Jesus lives we shall live also. Death is not the end; it is the gateway to glory. Death is not farewell; it is the beginning of God's tomorrow.

My body will wear out, but I will have a new body in the new Jerusalem. I will also have a new name, new robe, new mansion and then a thousand years from now, I will be shouting on the hills of glory in my glorified, disease-free body. Life has no limits.

Jabez prayed: "Oh that you would bless me indeed!"

Jabez prayed for God's blessing.

What is the blessing? The blessing is the impartation of the supernatural power of God into a human life by the spoken Word of God's delegated authority.

Words have life and power. Words spoken under the anointing shape the destiny of individuals, families and nations. The first thing God did after creating Adam and Eve, was to bless them (Genesis 1:28) "And God blessed them and said to them… be fruitful and multiply... subdue [spiritual warfare]… and take dominion" [take charge over your life or someone else will].

God blessed Abraham in Genesis 12, "I will bless those that bless you…" Jewish fathers and mothers bless their children every Friday at Sabbath. They do this because of the supernatural power of the blessing. Their children go out and live their lives without limit, because their parents bless them with the blessing of Abraham.

Jacob blessed his twelve sons on his deathbed. Everything that Jacob spoke into the lives of his sons came true. The power of the blessing followed those boys until the last day of their lives. When a spiritual authority speaks the blessing over you, no person can steal or stop your blessing. Satan himself cannot stop God's blessing for you.

God's blessing and His abundance is limited only by us, not His resources, power or willingness. God wants to give to you but cannot unless you ask for His blessing.

God's provision is in His promises!

2 Peter 1:2, "Grace and peace be multiplied to you in the knowledge of God as

His divine power has given us all things that pertain to life." God has already given to you "all things that we need for life", but if you have not asked for it, it will sit in heaven wasted.

God's provision is for everyone. 2 Corinthians 9:8, "And God is able to make all grace abound towards you, that you always having all sufficiency in all things, may have an abundance for every good work."

The power of proclamation in receiving God's provision!

The prayer of Jabez is a proclamation. I encourage you to pray it each morning and evening, in faith, to live a life spiritually, emotionally, and financially without limit.

The word "proclaim" comes from the

Latin meaning to "shout forth." Proclamation is spiritual warfare, and it releases God's Word into our personal battle.

Isaiah 55:11, "So shall My Word be that goes forth from My mouth; it shall not return to Me void. But it shall accomplish which I please and it shall prosper in the thing where to I sent it."

In Hebrews 3:1 Jesus Christ is called, "The high priest of our profession."

Look at the power of God's spoken word (Genesis 1:3), "And God said let there be light and there was light;" God didn't think it or meditate on it, He spoke it. Psalm 33:6, "By the word of the Lord the heavens were made... and all the hosts of them by the breath of His mouth."

Revelation 19 says that when Jesus

returns to earth at Armageddon, out of His mouth shall come a two-edged sword with which He shall smite the nations of the world.

How is the power of God released into your life? The power of God is released through the spoken Word of God. As powerful as God is, He cannot answer prayer until you pray. He does not answer a petition that has not been presented.

The second thing Moses did was to take hold of the rod. It became a spiritual weapon. Psalm 149:5-9, "Let the saints be joyful in glory, let them sing aloud upon their beds. Let the high praises of God be on their mouth, and a two-edged sword in their hand, to execute vengeance on the nations, and punishments on the people to bind their kings with chains and their nobles with fetters of iron; to execute on them the written judgment. This honor have all His saints."

Moses learned to stretch out his rod. You must learn to use your authority which is the spoken Word of God. Learn to make scriptural proclamations. In moments of doubt or fear about the future, declare this scriptural proclamation in Jeremiah 29, "For I know the plans I have for you, declares the Lord, plans to prosper you and not to harm you, plans to give you hope and a future."

Do you need self-defense from sickness? Make the proclamation of Psalm 118:17, "I shall not die but live, and declare the works of the Lord." You need to say: By His stripes I am now being healed because He is the Lord that heals all of my diseases; The angel of the Lord encamps round about me, no plague shall come nigh my dwelling; I confess that the Word of God is life and health to my flesh; I receive divine health now in the name of Jesus.

The Word of God can be self-defense from attack. You can confess through the name of Jesus Christ that, "no weapon formed against me shall prosper, and every tongue that rises against me in judgment I shall condemn. This is the heritage of the servants of the Lord, and their righteousness is from me". Deuteronomy 33:27, "The eternal God is your refuge, and underneath are the everlasting arms; He will thrust out the enemy before you and will shout, Destroy him!"

The Word of God is a proclamation in financial need. Joshua 1:8 declares, "This book of the law shall not depart from your mouth…for then shall you make your way prosperous and then you will have good success."

3 John 2, "Beloved I wish above all things that you mayest prosper and be in good health even as your soul prospereth."

It is God's will for you to be successful and blessed in all that you do. Take authority as a believer, and proclaim His Word for your needs.

MASTERING YOUR MONEY

Chapter 5

We live in a time when everyone needs wise financial counsel. Where can a person find sound financial advice? Not from the government! With a national debt racing past four trillion it would take more than two thousand years paying one million per day just to break even. The idea that Congress will balance the budget is a pipe dream.

You seldom get sound financial advice from relatives or friends. Only two percent of Americans are financially independent at the age of sixty-five. According to the Social Security Administration, eighty-five out of every one hundred Americans have less than two hundred and fifty dollars in their savings when they reach age sixty-five.

Where can you find sound financial advice? How would you like to own the most astute financial guide ever printed? Its wisdom and power defies anything Wall Street has ever published. It is time tested, and its proven financial principles are rock solid. It will teach you how to master your money and how to release God's power and wealth into your life.

What is the guide? The Bible.

The purpose of abundance is not to hoard it, but to share it

2 Corinthians 9:8, "...that you have abundance for every good work." Never in the New Testament is it written, "If we have enough money, we'll do it." Their plans didn't depend on money. They found the will of God. God provided for every good work.

One specific good work is to provide a dwelling place for God on Earth

We often talk as if the ultimate is to get to heaven, but it's clear in Scripture that the ultimate is to get heaven to earth. In the final chapters of Revelation, God brings heaven down to earth. Revelation 21:2, "Then I, John, saw the

Holy City, the new Jerusalem, coming down out of heaven from God, and God Himself will be with them and be their God."

The fact is that from the creation in Genesis to the closing scenes of Revelation, it is God's objective to dwell with man. Look at the tabernacle. God provided in advance all the gold and silver necessary to build the tabernacle. The tabernacle would cost in excess of one hundred million dollars in today's currency. Every piece of furniture, fabric, gold, silver and brass was designed with exact detail. It was of the highest quality.

In Genesis 15:13-14, God said to Abraham, "Know certainly that your descendants will be strangers in a country not their own, and will serve them, and they will afflict them four hundred years... and also the nation whom they serve I will judge; afterward they shall come out with great possessions."

Was it just for the Israelites to plunder the Egyptians? Yes. God had been keeping records for four hundred years; Jews worked as slaves. They collected their wages that day plus interest. God will not allow the Devil to steal your wages.

God gave them wealth for a purpose: to build the tabernacle. He wanted to live there in the Holy of Holies.

Exodus 25:4-5, "And Moses spoke… whoever is of a willing heart let him bring it as an offering to the Lord." In the Old Testament, tithes were never used to build churches. Churches were built with freewill offerings. The tithe was demanded. The point here is that if you take God's money (tithe) and build God's house, what have you given to God? Nothing.

What was the result of Moses' freewill offering? Exodus 36:5-6, "The people bring much more than enough… so Moses gave a commandment and the people were restrained from bringing too much." That seldom happens in the American church.

God's desire is to dwell with man. Let us consider Solomon's temple. David began as a shepherd boy, and at his death he gave approximately one hundred million to build the temple. Every detail of the temple was exact. Solomon's temple was majestic. The elders of the church (1 Chronicles 29:6) gave one hundred twenty-five million to build the temple plus one hundred million that came from King David.

Consider God's provision for you because your body is the temple of the Holy Spirit. 1 Corinthians 3:16-17, "Do you not know that you are the temple of

God and that the Spirit of God dwells in you? If anyone defiles the temple of God… God will destroy him. For the temple of God is Holy." Your body is the dwelling place of the Holy Spirit.

God wants to bless you with abundance that would stagger your mind if you have the faith to practice God's principles of health and prosperity. Remember you must GIVE your way to wealth.

Many people do not get a blessing because they did not thank God for the last one

I Thessalonians 5:18, "In everything give thanks, for this is the will of God in Christ Jesus concerning you."

Romans 1 showed that the refusal to be thankful brings God's judgment:

"They were not thankful, God gave them over to a reprobate mind." They believed a lie and were damned.

Are you thankful? Thanksgiving is caught, not taught. Thanksgiving is not an emotion; it is a decision, an act of your will. Thanksgiving begins with Thanks-living. Life is God's gift to you; what you do with that life is your gift to God.

Thank God for your talents by accepting them as obligations to be invested in the Kingdom of God. Use your opportunities as a challenge to achieve the impossible. Thank God for each new day and live it as if it were your last one.

You will discover that the spirit of Thanksgiving is the key to releasing the supernatural power of God, that your prayers may be answered and that supernatural provisions will explode in your life. Thanksgiving is a direct command from God to every believer, "Be thankful unto Him and bless His name."

Colossians 3:15, "And let the peace of God rule your hearts… and be thankful… and whatsoever you do in word or deed, do all in the name of Jesus Christ giving thanks to God the Father by Him."

God is too loving to be unkind and too wise to make a mistake. When you are not giving thanks to God, you are in open rebellion against God. Do you complain? What you do not have is to fault God's provision. Where you are in life is to fault God's leadership. Who you are is to fault the sovereignty of God.

Why doesn't God give you more? If you are not thankful for what you have, you will not be given more. The spirit of Thanksgiving is a decision. The spirit of Thanksgiving reflects the presence of the

Holy Spirit in you. Ephesians 5:19, "Speaking to yourselves in psalms, hymns and spiritual songs, singing and making melody in your heart to the Lord. Giving thanks always unto God the Father in the name of our Lord Jesus Christ." Spirit-filled people are thankful people.

The spirit of Thanksgiving is necessary to make other forms of prayer effective. Philippians 4:6, "Be anxious about nothing, but in everything by prayer and supplication and thanksgiving let your requests be made known unto God." Start your prayer time with Thanksgiving, not a series of bellyaches. Thanksgiving is the key to releasing God's supernatural power in your life.

Investing in the Kingdom of God is the only financially sure thing on planet Earth

2 Chronicles 26:5, "As long as he sought the Lord, God made him to prosper." A greater financial genius than John Rockefeller asks you to invest in His kingdom. He will give you a thirty, sixty, one hundred fold harvest. Every offering is an opportunity for you to increase your income.

Money is a great servant, but a terrible master

In Luke 12:15, Jesus said, "Take heed and beware of covetousness. For a man's life does not consisteth in the abundance of things which he possesseth."

Do you own your house, or does your house own you? Do you own your car, or does your car own you? Do not let your possessions take control of your life.

If you have not received anything, it is because you have not given anything

Proverbs 22:9, "He that hath a bountiful eye shall be blessed, for he giveth of his bread to the poor." The Bible says to give and it will be given unto you. What have you given?

Blessing Israel brings great prosperity

The future of the world will be determined by what happens in Jerusalem. Jerusalem holds the key to world peace. "Pray for the peace of Jerusalem; they shall prosper that love thee." (Psalm 122:6) Jerusalem holds the key to your prosperity.

Through John Hagee Ministries, Christians are joining forces with the Jewish people to rescue Jews from all around the world who wish to relocate to Israel. To date, John Hagee Ministries has donated in excess of $3.7 million sponsoring the transportation expenses for over 6,000 people. We have done this with the generous help of our partners throughout the Western Hemisphere.

With the collapse of Communism and the emergence of democracy, anti-Semitic political groups are on the rise, joining with anti-democratic forces in urging a return to a more closed society. Now with the world in chaos, the environment is more hostile towards Jews than ever and they are in clear and present danger.

As Christians, we must recognize the critical importance of the Jewish people in God's plan for us all. We must, in direct fulfillment of Jeremiah's prophecy, help bring God's people home to Israel.

Will you help us do more? Call 210-494-3900 to help.